THE WEATHER DETECTIVES

BY MARK EUBANK

ILLUSTRATED BY MARK A. HICKS

Gibbs Smith, Publisher
Salt Lake City

For my grandchildren who love exciting weather —M. E.

For the students in Mrs. Hicks's classroom —M. H.

First Edition
08 07 06 05 04   5 4 3 2 1

Disclaimer: Children should have adult supervision when performing the activities and experiments in this book. The publisher and author assume no responsibility for any damages or injuries incurred from partici- pating in any of the activities and experiments described herein.

Published by
Gibbs Smith, Publisher
P.O. Box 667
Layton, Utah 84041

Orders: 1.800.748.5439
www.gibbs-smith.com

Designed by Dawn DeVries Sokol
Printed and bound in Hong Kong

Library of Congress Cataloging-in-Publication Data

Eubank, Mark E.
  The weather detectives : fun-filled facts, experiments, and activities
  for kids / Mark Eubank ; illustrations by Mark A. Hicks. — 1st ed.
  p. cm.
Summary: Three children take a journey to Mars and Venus, encountering
  various meteorological phenomena along the way. Includes weather-related
  experiments and other activities.

ISBN 1-58685-412-7

  1. Weather—Experiments—Juvenile literature. [1. Weather. 2. Weather—
Experiments. 3. Experiments.] I. Hicks, Mark A., ill. II. Title.
QC981.3 .E88 2004
551.5'078—dc22

                         2003021032

CONTENTS

INTRODUCTION

MEET BRYAN BRONSON, the youngest astronaut ever selected to travel to Mars. Bryan won first place in the world science fair and was awarded a space travel scholarship. He and his two best friends, Rudy and Olivia, get to travel into outer space! But the adventure doesn't stop there. Bryan and his friends have a series of adventures, from surviving a tornado to escaping an avalanche. The friends decide to form a club and record their adventures and discoveries. They call themselves the Weather Detectives.

Chapter 1

ATMOSPHERE
AND WEATHER

FROM OUTER SPACE, Earth looks like a blue-green marble. There is no other place in the universe like it that we know about. The Hubble Telescope has looked at thousands of stars and planets and moons but has never seen anything like Earth.

Planet Earth usually has a 50 percent cloud cover. This is the part of Earth's atmosphere where rain and snow come from. From down on the ground it looks like the clouds are really high up, but compared to the size of Earth, the clouds are really low. Earth's weather layer is called the troposphere (TROW-puh-sfeer), and it is very thin compared to the size of Earth. Besides giving us clouds and rain and wind, and making our temperatures nice, the atmosphere protects us from harmful ultraviolet rays from the sun. It even protects us from small meteors that otherwise would crash into Earth! Think of Earth's atmosphere like the skin of an apple. It isn't very thick, but it protects the apple from bugs and storms and even too much sunshine.

In this book you will learn how Earth's atmosphere makes weather with the water cycle, clouds, wind, rain, and snow.

EXPERIMENT

Cut an apple in half. Look at the skin of the apple from the outside. Can you tell how thick the skin is? Now look at the inside of the apple and notice how thin the skin layer is compared to the rest of the apple. This is about how thin Earth's weather layer is compared to the rest of the earth. Now you can eat the apple.

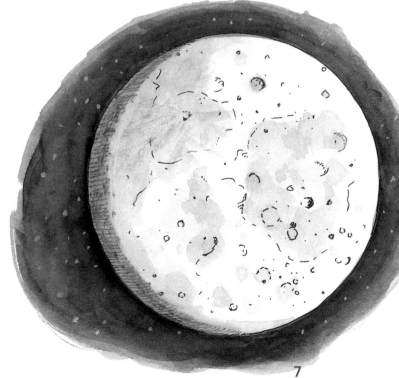

FACT:

The moon doesn't have an atmosphere, so there is no weather there. Many of the planets in our solar system have an atmosphere and they have weather, but it doesn't mean it's the same kind of atmosphere or weather we have on Earth.

KILLER RAIN

Venus, the second planet from the sun, is covered with clouds and reflects much of the sunlight. This makes the planet appear very bright from outer space. Venus has strong weather systems. Lightning bolts are common and so are thick clouds. But the rain is not the kind you would want to be in . . .

As Bryan, Olivia, and Rudy approached Venus, Olivia exclaimed, "It looks like it's raining cats and dogs down there!"

"Maybe, but it's not a rainstorm we would want to be in," said Bryan.

"Why not?" asked Olivia.

Bryan explained, "The clouds on Venus are made of sulfuric acid, so any rain would eat right through your space suit. And the temperatures are more than 800 degrees Fahrenheit at the surface. That would fry us to a crisp."

Olivia knew it was hot on the surface of Venus, but she didn't know it was *that* hot!

The spaceship finished the flyby tour of Venus and headed back toward Earth, then on to Mars.

ATTACK OF THE MARTIAN SANDSTORM

As the spacecraft neared Mars, the red planet, Bryan, Rudy, and Olivia could easily see the ground. The atmosphere on Mars is very thin. There were some clouds near the top and bottom of the

planet, but most areas were very clear. The spacecraft set down near the edge of a large canyon. Soon the kids and the other astronauts were all in their space suits and were out on the surface of Mars.

Olivia and Rudy were going to help Bryan with his weather experiments. They quickly set up a weather station that would measure temperature and wind and record the data in a computer.

"Be careful with the anemometer" (an-ee-MOM-uh-ter), Bryan told them.

"Which instrument is the anemometer," asked Rudy?

"It's the one with the three cups on the top," answered Bryan. "That's the one that turns

if there is any wind and measures how strong it is."

After they got the weather station set up, the other astronauts went off to gather rock samples while Bryan took a high-tech thermometer and went to measure the

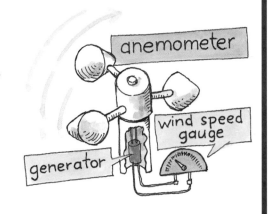

As the wind turns the cups, a shaft attached to the cups turns a small generator. The generator makes a small amount of electricity, and the electricity is converted to a wind speed reading. The faster the wind, the more electricity, and the higher the wind reading.

temperature in various places. Some distance away was a mountain with what looked like a dry streambed leading to a big canyon. As Bryan measured the temperatures, he discovered the air in the dry streambed was colder than the air in the higher areas. Bryan knew that cold air is heavier than warm air. He calculated the cold air was flowing down the streambed toward the canyon just as water would.

Bryan looked up and saw what seemed to be a red cloud in the distance. He walked to the top of a small hill where he could see the horizon better. It was then that he realized they might all be in trouble! Bryan contacted Olivia and Rudy over his headset. "Hey! We've got to get back to the lander right away."

"What's wrong?" Rudy asked.

"We've got a bad dust storm coming. It may be so thick that we won't be able to see our way back, so we need to get going right now."

"Are we going to be okay?" Rudy asked fearfully.

Bryan estimated the storm was at least ten miles away, and it was traveling about twenty miles per hour, so they had about thirty minutes

EXPERIMENT

Take off your shoes and socks and stand directly in front of your refrigerator. Stand there for at least 15 seconds and try to determine if your forehead or your feet are warmer. Now open the refrigerator door and stand right in front of it again. What do you feel where your feet are? Are they getting colder?

The refrigerator is full of cold air (usually around 35 degrees). Because cold air is heavier than warm air, you will feel it rush down over your feet.

before it hit. "We'll be fine," he said, "as long as we head back right now."

Soon they were all safely back at the lander. "Stow all the rocks in the rock boxes and let's prepare for takeoff!" Bryan exclaimed.

As they left the surface of Mars, they could all see the big sandstorm coming. It was huge! It covered the horizon and extended from the surface of Mars to thousands of feet above. It was like a wall of red sand. They barely escaped!

The formula for measuring how fast a storm will reach you is Distance = Rate x Time. The time is calculated by dividing the distance by the rate (Time = Distance ÷ Rate). Bryan estimated that the distance was 10 miles and estimated the storm was traveling at 20 miles per hour. Dividing 10 miles by 20 miles per hour gives .5 hours, or 30 minutes.

FACT:

Sandstorms on Mars can have winds of more than 40 miles per hour. Now that's fast!

FACT:

Sand and dust on Mars are red, not brown like sand and dust on Earth. The surface of Mars has a lot of iron in it. The iron makes the sand an orange-reddish color just like rust. It's like the red sand found in the Namibian Desert in southwest Africa or like the red sandstone spires at Bryce Canyon National Park in Utah.

Chapter 2
WATER CYCLE
AND RAIN

WHAT IS THE WATER CYCLE?

As the sun shines on Earth, water evaporates from the oceans. The warm, moist air rises until the water vapor cools and becomes visible as clouds. Winds blow the clouds over the continents where it rains and snows. The melting snow and rainwater run down the rivers, back to the ocean where the process starts over again. That's the water cycle.

BRYAN AND THE WEATHER DETECTIVES landed at the Space Port in Florida. "Florida has some very interesting weather," Bryan said. "Especially during hurricane season. Why don't we stay here for a while?"

"You mean we're going to stay here during hurricane season *on purpose?*" Rudy wailed.

Bryan winked at Olivia. "Sure, why not?" he asked.

"How else can we be weather detectives if we don't investigate the weather?" Olivia added.

The friends sat down by the motel pool to plan their stay. Suddenly Rudy noticed how uncomfortable he was feeling. "It feels hotter here than being in my space suit on a long space walk," he said.

Olivia looked over at the thermometer by the pool and said, "It's only 82 degrees, but it sure feels hotter, doesn't it?"

Bryan chimed in, "It feels extra hot because the humidity is going up."

"Why would that make it feel hotter?" asked Rudy.

Bryan explained, "There is always water vapor in the air. The vapor is made of little water droplets that are invisible. Sometimes there are more droplets than other times. This vapor is also called *humidity*. When the air is dry, the moisture on our skin evaporates and helps us stay comfortable, but when the humidity is high, the evaporation doesn't work nearly as well and we feel sticky and uncomfortable."

All of a sudden, a large, dark cloud

HOW DO THERMOMETERS WORK?

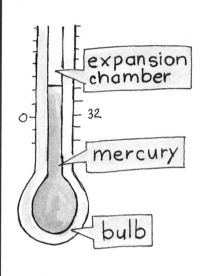

Most thermometers are made with mercury. When the mercury gets hot it expands (gets bigger) and rises inside a glass tube. The higher the temperature, the higher the mercury goes. The lower the temperature, the lower it goes. Mercury is poisonous, but it is safe when contained in the glass of a thermometer.

moved in front of the sun and it started to rain. Not just little drops, but great big, fat raindrops. The three of them dashed into the motel lobby and watched in amazement as the sudden storm pounded the area.

"It'll be over in about 15 minutes," said the motel manager.

"How do you know?" asked Rudy.

"Happens all the time," the manager said. "The morning starts off sunny and nice, then all of a sudden the clouds start developing, real quick-like, and wham, you've got a cloudburst."

They watched the rain hitting in torrents. Water was running everywhere. Most of it headed into a little stream and ran into the ocean. Sure enough, in about 15 minutes it was over. The sun was back out and

they move from west to east."

"Is that bad?" asked Rudy.

"No, it just means something unusual is going on," answered Bryan.

"Like . . . like what?" stammered Rudy.

"Well," said Bryan, "I've been noticing the way the waves have been getting bigger all day, and with those clouds coming from that direction, I think we have a hurricane approaching!"

the storm had moved away. As they went back out by the pool, Bryan told them they had just seen a miniature version of the water cycle on earth.

HURRICANE BOB

Later that afternoon Bryan noticed some high, thin, wispy clouds moving overhead. What caught his attention was the direction they were moving.

"What are you looking at?" asked Rudy.

"See those cirrus (SEAR-us) clouds? They are moving to the west. Normally

Evaporation EXPERIMENT

Take a piece of dark-colored construction paper and put one drop of water in the middle of the paper. Write down the time when you put the drop on the paper. Write down the time when the wet spot on the paper is completely gone. How long did it take for the water to evaporate? Where did the water go?

The water evaporated into the air as vapor.

Condensation EXPERIMENT

With the supervision of an adult, put an inch of water in a cooking pot. Put the pot on the stove and heat it on medium heat for about 5 minutes or until you see steam coming up from the pot. Next take a metal bowl and fill it with ice cubes from your freezer. Wearing thick gloves, carefully hold the bowl full of ice about one foot above the pan of boiling water. What starts to happen on the outside of the metal bowl is called *condensation*.

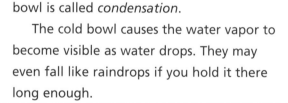

1 foot

The cold bowl causes the water vapor to become visible as water drops. They may even fall like raindrops if you hold it there long enough.

"Oh, no!" wailed Rudy. "Let's get out of here."

"Let's turn on the TV weather report and see what they say," Bryan suggested.

Sure enough, the TV weatherman showed a satellite picture of a hurricane coming from the east. They called it Hurricane Bob, and it was heading right toward them! The winds were over 120 miles per hour. It was a Category 3 hurricane.

The weatherman said Hurricane Bob was expected to become a Category 4 by morning. Now Rudy was getting really afraid. Bryan told him if they all followed the safety rules they would have the best chance of staying safe.

"Olivia, why don't you tell our driver to take the car down to the gas station and fill it up with gasoline," Bryan said. "If we lose power for a long time, the pumps at the gas station might not work for days. Rudy, why don't you go to the store and

cirrus

cumulus

stratus

Types of Clouds

There are three main groups of clouds. High clouds, middle clouds, and low clouds. High clouds are called cirrus (SEAR-us). Middle clouds are called cumulus (KEWM-yuh-luhs). Low clouds are called stratus (str-A-tus). The high clouds are made of ice crystals and are rather wispy looking. The middle clouds look like cotton and are fluffy. The low clouds are spread out and gray. Fog is an example of low clouds.

Hurricanes

Category	Sustained Wind	Damage to Well-Built Buildings
Category 1	74–95 mph	minimal
Category 2	96–110 mph	moderate
Category 3	111–130 mph	extensive
Category 4	131–155 mph	extreme
Category 5	over 155 mph	catastrophic

get some canned food, a couple of flashlights, and a portable radio. I'll help the motel manager bring in all the patio furniture and help him board up the windows so they won't get broken by flying objects."

Everyone took off in different directions to get everything done. Bryan helped the manager wedge wood into the frames of the sliding glass doors that were in the lobby so they wouldn't lift out of their tracks in the high wind. He suggested the manager fill his bathtub with water so he would have drinking water for several days if the city water went out. He also suggested he turn up the refrigerator to maximum cold and not open it unless it was necessary. That way his food would last longer if the power went out.

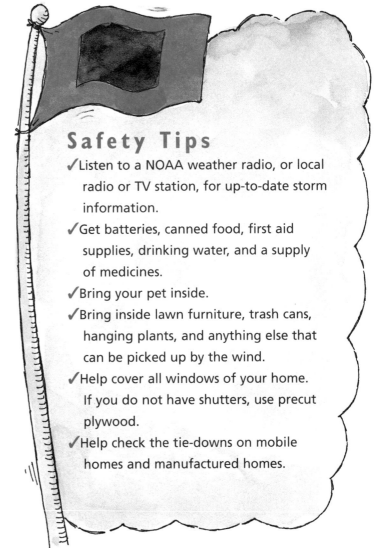

Safety Tips

✓ Listen to a NOAA weather radio, or local radio or TV station, for up-to-date storm information.

✓ Get batteries, canned food, first aid supplies, drinking water, and a supply of medicines.

✓ Bring your pet inside.

✓ Bring inside lawn furniture, trash cans, hanging plants, and anything else that can be picked up by the wind.

✓ Help cover all windows of your home. If you do not have shutters, use precut plywood.

✓ Help check the tie-downs on mobile homes and manufactured homes.

ACTIVITY: Make Your Own Rain Gauge

You will need:

- a large straight-walled can such as a 46-ounce juice can or Crisco can
- a small straight-walled jar like an olive jar or tall medicine container
- ruler
- paper
- tape
- pencil

You will use the can and the jar to amplify the rain so you can make very accurate readings of the rainfall.

If the lid is still sealed to the can, remove it with a can opener.

Make sure the can is clean, then pour enough water into the can to cover the bottom *exactly* one-half inch. Measure this very carefully with a ruler.

Tape a strip of paper on the outside of the jar from the top to the bottom. Put a mark on the paper at the exact bottom of the inside of the jar.

Now, pour the water from the can into the jar.

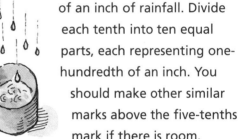

Mark the paper at the top of the water level, then pour out the water. (The top mark will represent one-half inch of rainfall, although it will not measure one-half inch with a ruler.)

Using the ruler, divide the distance between the two marks into five equal parts, each representing one-tenth of an inch of rainfall. Divide each tenth into ten equal parts, each representing one-hundredth of an inch. You should make other similar marks above the five-tenths mark if there is room.

Set the can outside in a level position away from tall buildings and trees. After it rains, pour the water from the can into the small jar and read the highest level. If there is more rain than the jar can measure, fill it to the highest mark and record the value. Then empty the jar and fill it again. Repeat until you have measured all the water from the can.

Add all the values together to get the total rainfall.

That's over 43 feet!

weather FACT:

Wettest place on earth
523.6 inches of rain each
year (29-year average)
Lloro, Colombia,
South America

Soon Rudy and Olivia were back. Rudy had gotten the supplies Bryan suggested. He had also bought some dog food for the manager's dog, Fluffy, who was now safely inside and curled up on a pillow. "There is one more thing I want to do," said Bryan. "I want to make a rain gauge so we can see how much rain Bob brings us."

During the night the wind roared and the rain beat in waves on the motel. The building shuddered like their spaceship during takeoff, but they were all safe inside. Hurricane Bob had made a turn in the night, and the eye of the storm hit 200 miles north of them. Their area had very strong winds and lots of rain, but they had been lucky and missed the main part of the hurricane. The next morning Olivia went out to get the rain gauge. They couldn't believe it: 6.30 inches of rain had fallen overnight. What a storm!

Did you know seagulls fly inland just before a storm? Seagulls can live anywhere in the U.S., but the ones that live along the coastal areas will often leave the beaches and go inland up to a day before a storm.

Chapter 3
FREEZING RAIN

WHAT IS FREEZING RAIN?

When warm, moist air moves up and over low-level cold air, it can start raining into the colder air. As the warm raindrops reach the cold surface, they freeze on impact.

RUDY ON HIS REAR END

Bryan, Rudy, and Olivia next went to Huntsville, Alabama. It's called the Space Capital of America. They wanted to visit the U.S. Space & Rocket Center, where kids can attend Space Camp.

During the evening, the temperatures dropped way down to the 20s. "This is not normal," said Bryan.

"Oh, no!" Rudy wailed. "Not another hurricane."

"No," said Bryan, "not a hurricane. I think we are going to have freezing rain!"

"What do we do?" screeched Rudy.

Bryan said confidently, "We stay inside the motel tonight and hope the power stays on."

Sure enough it did start to rain. As the

kid detectives looked outside they could see the raindrops splashing down on the hoods of the cars. But with the surface temperatures below freezing, the drops of water quickly froze. They froze on everything they touched. The cars were getting icy. The trees were coated with ice and so were the power lines. They decided it was a good time to climb into their warm beds and go to sleep.

All night long it rained and everything was being covered with a glaze of ice. In the night they heard strange noises. There were sounds like a rifle going off as tree branches snapped under the weight of the ice. Power lines broke and the red glow from the clocks in their motel bedrooms suddenly went dark. When they awoke in the morning, their rooms were cold.

"Uh-oh," said Olivia to herself. "I think the power is still out." She flipped the light switch on and off . . . nothing.

When Rudy woke up, Bryan was already awake and dressed.

"Maybe we'd better go next door and check on Olivia," Rudy said. He went to the curtains and opened them to let some light in. Rudy couldn't believe his eyes.

"Look at this!" he shouted. There were tree limbs lying everywhere. Some of the power lines hung limp from their poles. And ice was everywhere. Rudy ran outside to look, and . . . SLAM! The next thing he knew, he was on his rear end! You couldn't even walk, it was so slippery.

"Are you all right?" Bryan asked.

"Yeah, but I sure didn't expect to fall down," sighed Rudy. The ice was at least an inch thick on everything. The entire area was like an ice-skating rink.

Ice is so heavy, it only takes one-half inch on the power lines to break them.

Sorry
Rudy.

Chapter 4

WIND

WHAT MAKES THE WIND BLOW?

Wind is air that is moving. When the air is calm, we say there is no wind. When the air is moving around quickly, we say it is very windy. Sunlight warms our planet, but not all areas get equally heated. This uneven heating causes different air pressures because in some areas the air is rising and in other areas the air is sinking. Air moves from high pressure areas to low pressure areas. The higher the difference between two pressures, the stronger the wind will be.

THE NEXT ADVENTURE of the Weather Detectives was in the suburbs of Kansas City, Missouri. They decided to take a trip there. The second morning they were there was sunny, mild, and beautiful. Olivia suggested the three friends buy some lunch and take it to a park.

They went to a pretty place called Hidden Valley Park where they ate cheeseburgers, french fries, and had fresh strawberries for dessert. Rudy was lying in the grass on his back watching the billowy clouds roll by. Gradually the wind picked up and started blowing the wrappers from their lunch around. Rudy ran to pick up the papers and put them in the trash. Olivia said, "The wind is getting pretty strong. I wonder how strong it is."

Bryan said, "It's around 25 miles per hour!"

"How do you know that?" questioned Olivia.

"Hear that noise?" Bryan asked. "Wind whistles in wires from 25 to 31 miles per hour, so I figure the wind must be at least 25 miles per hour."

UP, UP, AND AWAY

As they all lay there watching the clouds billow up, something caught their attention. It was a large, yellow hot air balloon. It looked like it would land in the park! They all jumped up and ran to where it was

Bryan Bronson's Wind Weather Facts

Steady Wind	Wind Effects
0–1 mph	Smoke rises vertically
2–3 mph	Direction of wind shown by smoke, but not by wind vanes
4–7 mph	Wind felt on face; leaves rustle; vanes begin to move
8–12 mph	Leaves and small twigs constantly moving; light flags extended
13–18 mph	Dust, leaves, and loose paper lifted; small tree branches move
19–24 mph	Small branches in trees begin to sway
25–31 mph	Larger tree branches moving; whistling in wires
32–38 mph	Whole trees moving; resistance felt walking against wind
39–46 mph	Twigs break off trees; difficulty felt walking against wind
47–54 mph	Slight structural damage occurs; shingles blown off roofs
55–63 mph	Trees broken or uprooted; structural damage occurs
64–72 mph	Not often experienced; accompanied by widespread damage
73+ mph	Rarely experienced; extensive damage occurs

What Is Altitude?

The height of an object above the surface (either of land or sea level).

coming down. Slowly the large balloon and its basket approached the ground. A man in the balloon threw out some ropes, and two men on the ground grabbed them and started pulling the balloon downward. Then Bryan saw the sign on a nearby truck: Balloon Rides $25. Bryan said, "Come on, let's take a ride. It will be a blast!"

Rudy said, "I don't know. It doesn't look safe." Rudy was always nervous.

"We've been to Mars and back in a rocket—surely we can ride in a hot air balloon!" exclaimed Olivia.

"You kids want a ride in my beautiful balloon?" the pilot asked them.

"Absolutely!" said Bryan, and they all climbed aboard.

Soon, they were up, up, and away. They could see all over the park. In fact, they could see the tall buildings off to the south-

How high can we go?

How far can we go?

How do we get down?

west in Kansas City. The winds had dropped off and they were going nearly straight up.

"How high are we now?" Bryan asked the pilot.

"Two thousand feet above the ground."

All of a sudden there was a roaring

EXPERIMENT

Get a large fruit jar with a screw-on lid. Fill it about one-third full of light vegetable oil. Now add water until it is about two-thirds full. Do the oil and water mix or stay separate? Make sure the lid is on tight and shake the jar hard. Now let the jar sit for 5 to 15 minutes. What happens?

The oil is like warm air: it is lighter and wants to rise. The water is like cold air: it is heavier and wants to stay near the bottom.

sound that startled Rudy. "What's that?!" he hollered.

"That's just the burners putting more hot air into the balloon," laughed the pilot. "Warm air is lighter than cold air so it wants to rise. That's what is taking us up," he explained.

In ten more minutes they were five thousand feet above the ground and it was starting to feel a little chilly.

Rudy spotted it first. "Isn't that a little cloud forming?" he asked.

"Where?" asked Olivia.

"Right there, off to our left," the pilot answered. "The sun is heating the ground and warming the air near the surface of the earth. As it rises, it is cooling and the humidity is going up. At this altitude the water vapor in the air is just now starting to become visible. I'll bet we have clouds forming all over the place soon."

In another fifteen minutes there were little puffy clouds

weather FACT:

Dry air cools about five degrees for every thousand feet it rises. Moist air only cools about three degrees for every thousand feet.

developing everywhere.

"We should land pretty soon," said Bryan. "I've got a feeling these clouds are just the beginning."

As the pilot landed the balloon back in the park, the three friends jumped onto solid ground. Olivia was laughing softly to herself.

"What's so funny?" Rudy asked.

"I just think it's funny that we had a weather adventure *without* it turning into a weather disaster!"

EXPERIMENT: Does Warm Air Rise?

Cut an 8-inch diameter circle out of a piece of paper.

With a pencil, start in the center of the circle and draw a spiral out from the center. Keep going around until you reach the outer edge.

Carefully take scissors and, starting on the outer edge of the paper, cut along the spiral line almost all the way to the center.

Take a thread and attach it to the center. As you hold the thread, the spiral will hang down like a Christmas tree.

Have an adult help you take the lamp-shade off a table lamp. Turn the lamp on for a few minutes. The lightbulb will warm the air above it.

Now hold the spiral above the lightbulb so the lowest part is about two inches above the bulb. What is happening to the spiral? What does this prove?

The warm air rises and makes the spiral rotate. This shows warm air *does* rise!

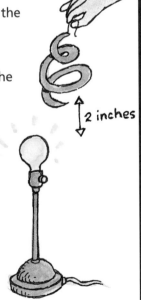

2 inches

Chapter 5

LIGHTNING

WHAT IS LIGHTNING?

Lightning is a giant spark of electricity in the sky. Electricity has two parts, a negative charge and a positive charge, just like on a battery. The electricity moves from the negative towards the positive. There is electricity in the sky but normally the charges are mixed up and balanced with no sparks. In a thunderstorm, the wind moves raindrops and ice crystals around and separates the electric charges. Some parts of the clouds end up with a lot of negative charges while the ground can have positive charges. If the difference between the two charges is big enough, a spark will jump between them to equalize things. This is what a lightning bolt is—a giant spark.

TWO HOURS AFTER their balloon ride, Bryan, Olivia, and Rudy were walking back to the motel. The sky was completely cloudy and the clouds were getting really dark in the west. Suddenly a jagged bolt of lightning stabbed down off to their right.

One one-thousand...

"One one-thousand, two one-thousand," Bryan started counting.

"What are you doing?" questioned Rudy.

"Three one-thousand, four one-thousand . . ." Bryan kept on counting.

The 30-30 Rule

If the sound of thunder is less than 30 seconds from when you see the flash of lightning, you need to go indoors. And you need to stay inside until 30 minutes after the last time you hear thunder.

Finally when he got to ten one-thousand, there was a deep rumbling boom of thunder. "I wanted to see how far away the lightning was," Bryan finally said. "The sound takes five seconds to go one mile. I counted ten seconds, so the lightning is two miles away."

weather FACT:

The light from lightning reaches your eyes instantly, but the sound from the thunder travels much more slowly. Sound takes five seconds to go one mile. So if you see lightning and then hear the sound of thunder five seconds later, that means the lightning was one mile away.

15 feet

If you are caught outside when lightning is striking, crouch down with your feet together. Cover your ears with your hands to prevent hearing damage from thunder. Stay 15 feet away from other people.

"Uh-oh," said Rudy, "I think we are in danger. I remember in flight school they told us if the time between the lightning flash and the thunder was less than thirty seconds we needed to be indoors."

"Let's go!" cried Olivia and Bryan at the same time, and they all took off running for the motel.

EXPERIMENT

Try walking and sliding your shoes across carpeting while holding a key or a coin between your thumb and forefinger. When you touch something metal with the metal object you are holding, you may see a little spark of electricity. This is a miniature version of lightning.

Simply Shocking!

Safety Tips for Lightning Storms

IF OUTSIDE
- ✓ Stay away from water.
- ✓ Stay away from high ground.
- ✓ Stay away from open space.
- ✓ Stay away from all metal objects, including electric wires, fences, machinery, and power tools.
- ✓ Do NOT seek shelter underneath a canopy, in a small covered picnic area, or near trees.
- ✓ DO seek shelter in a substantial building or inside a car, truck, or van with the windows completely rolled up.

IF INSIDE
- ✓ Stay away from water.
- ✓ Stay away from doors and windows.
- ✓ Do not use telephone.
- ✓ Take off headsets.
- ✓ Turn off, unplug, and stay away from appliances, computers, power tools, and televisions. (Lightning can strike electrical lines and phone lines outside and send shocks inside.)

Chapter 6
TORNADOES

THE THREE KIDS, out of breath, made it safely back to their motel. Just then they heard a siren. "Must be a fire somewhere," said Olivia.

"No way!" shouted Bryan. "That's not a fire siren—that's a *tornado* siren. We've got to take cover!"

The three of them ran to the main office

of the motel. The sky in the west was very dark, almost black, but with an eerie green look to it. Lightning bolts were flashing everywhere and the thunder was constant. It was the worst-looking storm Rudy had ever seen.

"Have you got a storm shelter?" Bryan asked the motel clerk.

"Sure do, and we're going to need it by the look of that sky. Follow me!" the clerk said. He led them to a flight of stairs that went down into a basement under the motel. The clerk turned on a dim lightbulb hanging on a black cord from the ceiling. "We can sit on those patio chairs," the clerk said, pointing to a stack of chairs in the corner. But nobody was sitting.

Rudy was pacing around like a caged tiger. "There are no windows down here," he kept saying.

"Wouldn't want a window, now would we?" drawled the clerk. "Somethin' like that could blow out and shower us with

WHAT IS DOPPLER RADAR?

When you go to a canyon and yell, you can hear an echo back off the canyon wall. Radar is very similar, but rather than hollering, it sends out a burst of radio waves. When these waves bounce back off a raindrop or snowflake, the distance to it can be determined. So radar can tell how far away storms are. A special kind of radar called Doppler radar can also determine how fast the raindrops are moving. In this way, it can tell what the winds are like in a storm.

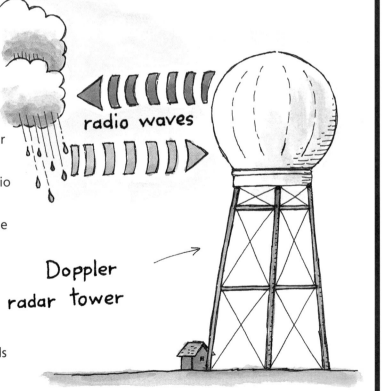

radio waves

Doppler radar tower

glass in a storm like this." Rudy knew he was right, but he still wanted to see what was going on outside.

"Do you have a radio down here in the basement?" Bryan asked the clerk.

"Better than that. I got a little TV over in the corner."

Rudy ran to the corner, found the TV, and turned it on. The TV weatherman was showing not just one storm but a line of severe storms. They were moving out of Kansas and into Missouri. "This storm is especially strong," said the weatherman, "and it's moving over the northeast part of Kansas City."

"That's right where we are!" yelled the clerk.

The TV weatherman continued, "Our latest Doppler image shows a low-level wind shear with a ground lock two miles west of Hidden Valley Park. This could be a tornado, folks, so take shelter."

"Oh, no! That's *right* where we are!" yelled the clerk.

"Oh, no!" cried Rudy. "What do we do?"

TIPS FOR TORNADO SAFETY

✓ Take cover. Find a shelter or sturdy concrete basement.

✓ Move close to the walls in case something from the floor above crashes through the ceiling.

✓ Keep a flashlight and a battery-powered radio in case the power goes out.

✓ If you can't get underground, go to an inside hallway at the lowest level or get under a piece of sturdy furniture (like a workbench, heavy table, or desk). Or drag a mattress off a bed, get in the bathtub, and cover yourself with the mattress.

✓ If there is no time to get indoors, lie in a ditch or a low-lying area or crouch near a strong building.

✓ If in a car, get out immediately and take shelter in a nearby building.

Suddenly a huge boom sounded outside.

"Wha . . . wha . . . what's that?" cried Rudy.

"Can't be sure," answered the clerk. "Could be some close lightning strikes with really loud thunder, or it could be something big and heavy hitting the motel." Just then there was an especially loud thump and the lightbulb on the ceiling started swaying back and forth.

"What was that?!" shrieked Rudy.

"I don't know," answered the motel clerk, "but I didn't like the sound of it."

A huge crash sounded and the entire building shuddered. Then the light and the TV went out and the room was plunged into darkness! Rudy tried to scream, but he was so frightened no sounds came out. They all just sat there in the dark, not knowing what to think. When Bryan finally spoke, it startled them. "Sounds pretty quiet up there now," he said.

Just then a dim light came on. "Good thing I brought this flashlight along," said the motel clerk. "Let's go upstairs and look around."

The clerk took the lead and tried to open the door back up into the motel, but it was stuck. "Give me a hand with this," he said to the kids. They put their shoulders to the door and pushed with all of their might. Something was blocking the door, but they were slowly able to open it. "That's the candy vending machine!" exclaimed the clerk as he looked down. "It used to be up against the wall over by the desk. I guess . . ." and then he stopped in mid-sentence as he looked into the motel lobby. He couldn't believe his eyes.

The roof was gone and there in the middle of the lobby was a pickup truck and a car! The car was upside down and leaning crazily against what used to be the check-in counter. The pickup truck was on top of the car with the front of the truck pointing toward the sky. There were pieces of broken glass and metal everywhere. All the windows were broken. The walls were still up on two sides of the building, but they were swaying gently back and forth.

"So this is what a tornado can do," said Olivia.

They carefully picked their way through the lobby. They didn't have to go through the door because the entire wall with the door was gone. They just walked out where the door used to be and into the parking lot. The sky was clearing and there were whole trees and tree limbs scattered on the ground everywhere. The big motel sign had crashed to the ground.

Rudy was still speechless until he picked up something. "What's that?" asked Bryan.

"I don't know for sure," answered Rudy. "It looks like a school book." He opened the cover. "*Developing Skills in Algebra,*

Property of Emporia High School," Rudy read slowly. "Is there an Emporia High School around here?" he asked.

"No," answered the clerk. "Emporia is in Kansas and we're in Missouri."

"It's more than a hundred miles away," said Bryan. "The tornado must have picked up that book in Emporia and carried it along in the storm until it landed here."

"Is that even possible?" Olivia asked.

"Well, it doesn't happen very often," answered Bryan, "but I've heard of it happening before."

"Well, I'll be darned," said the motel clerk. "I thought I had seen everything."

"Who would have thought we would live to survive a tornado!" exclaimed Olivia.

"I don't know how exciting it is," grumbled Rudy. "Even if we survived the tornado, it almost scared me to death."

"I've heard of a worse experience with a tornado," said Bryan. "My Grandpa Bronson was actually inside the center of a tornado and lived to tell about it!"

"What?!" exclaimed Olivia and Rudy.

"I have a letter from him explaining," Bryan said. "He sent it to me after I told him about our Weather Detectives club. I've just been waiting for a good time to read it to you."

"Well, no time like the present!" Rudy said.

EXPERIMENT

To see what a tornado looks like, get an empty, clear plastic two-liter soda pop bottle. Carefully remove the plastic label. Fill the bottle with water. Add a few drops of red food coloring and some red glitter. Hold the bottle, upside down, over the sink and swirl the bottle around and around in small circles. Stop swirling the bottle and just hold it over the sink. As the water comes out of the bottle, there will be water inside the bottle rotating rapidly in a circular motion. This is called a vortex. If it doesn't work, try it again. This is what a tornado looks like.

Cool experiment!

Grandpa Bronson's Great Tornado Adventure

Dear Bryan and Friends:

I was very glad to hear about your Weather Detectives Club. There's nothing so interesting as the weather. Let me tell you about the time I was down in Kansas.

Back then I was working at a car dealership, and one summer day we heard on the radio that there was a tornado watch for our area. Now a watch means you keep your eyes open and pay attention to the weather. It doesn't mean anything is going to happen right now, but it could later. A couple of us went outside and looked around. All we saw were blue skies. It didn't look bad to us, so we went back inside.

Later that afternoon there were some clouds around, but that's how it is in Kansas, so we didn't pay much attention. Then the music on the radio stopped and the announcer came on and said there was a tornado warning for our area! Well, I didn't want to miss the excitement, so I ran outside with a couple of my buddies. We looked around and there was a dark cloud down in the southwest. One of the guys said that was probably the tornado and they all scattered for cover. But me, I stayed put. I wanted to be sure.

As I kept looking at that big, dark cloud, I did see a tornado, but it was just a little one. I walked out to the sidewalk to get a better look at it, and it didn't seem to be moving. It didn't go left, and it didn't go right, but it did get bigger. About that time I realized it was probably coming straight at me! That's why it looked bigger. I ran back to the car dealership, but they had locked the doors! Can you imagine that? I guess they didn't want the doors to blow open in the storm. Well there I was, stuck outside, so I took my fists and beat on the door. Bam, bam, bam! "Let me in! Let me in!" I hollered, but nobody could hear me.

The wind was gettin' really strong now and I could see this big, black twister just across town. Well, I figured I'd just borrow one of the cars on the car lot and drive away real fast like. I jumped in a car, but there were no keys! They usually kept keys in the cars on the lot, but that car didn't have any. I ran to another car and checked to see if it had keys before I jumped in. It did have keys, and boy was I glad! I sat down and cranked on the starter. There was a rhhrur, rhhrur, rhhrur sound, but it wouldn't start. I tried it again and it went, click, click, click. That car wasn't going to take me anywhere. I was starting to get a little scared, but I knew I had to keep my wits about me. By now the tornado looked huge and it was just down the street. I knew I couldn't outrun it, but I had to do something.

There was a tree out by the curb that was probably thirty feet tall, and the trunk of the tree was about a foot in diameter. I ran over to the tree and laid down on the ground on my stomach with my feet out behind me. I faced the tornado so I could see it, then put my arms around the tree trunk and held on for dear life. Here it came, right across the street, this big wall of dirt and pieces of buildings and I don't know what all. There was a car parked across the street from where I was. All of a sudden the car lifted up and blew away! Then I felt my legs being lifted into the air! Then the storm threw me back down. Then it lifted me up again. I felt like I was going to lose my grip on the tree, but I held on for all I was worth. Up and down, up and down—the storm was banging me to the ground, then lifting me up. At one point, I felt like I was going to lose one of my shoes. I don't know why that bothered me, but I wiggled my foot trying to keep my shoe from flying away.

With a big whump, the tornado threw me flat again and then the wind relaxed. I got up and brushed myself off. There was dirt and junk all over me, but I was alive. I had just gone through a tornado and lived to tell about it. I was feeling pretty good until I looked around and realized . . . oh, no! I was on the inside of the tornado! If the front part had gone by, then the back half of the tornado must still be coming!

I went back to the tree, laid down again and held on for dear life. Sure enough, here came the back part of the tornado across the street and right toward me. The dirt started flying and so did I! Up and down it pulled me. The pull this time was really something. I started losing my grip on the tree, and finally it yanked me off and rolled me down the street. At that point I blacked out.

I don't know how long I was unconscious, but when I woke up I looked all around trying to see which way to run, but the tornado was gone. I was bruised and sore. I had mud in my eyes and little rocks in my ears, but I was alive! It had rolled me along for about one hundred feet. When I went back to the tree, guess what I found?

The tree was snapped right off about four feet above the ground. If I had been holding on any higher, I would have sailed away into the storm with the tree!

The tree after the storm!

Fujita Scale of Damage for Tornadoes

F Scale	Wind Speed	Type of Damage
F0	under 73 mph	Some damage to chimneys; breaks branches off trees; pushes over shallow-rooted trees; damages signboards
F1	73 to 112 mph	Peels surface off roofs; mobile homes pushed off foundations or overturned; moving autos pushed off roads; attached garages may be destroyed
F2	113 to 157 mph	Considerable damage; roofs torn off frame houses; mobile homes demolished; boxcars pushed over; large trees snapped or uprooted; light objects fly away like missiles
F3	158 to 206 mph	Roof and some walls torn off well-constructed buildings; trains overturned; most trees in forests uprooted
F4	207 to 260 mph	Well-constructed houses leveled; structures with weak foundations blown some distance; cars thrown through the air; large animals like cows become airborne
F5	261 to 318 mph	Strong frame houses lifted off foundations and carried considerable distances, eventually to disintegrate; automobile-sized missiles fly through the air in excess of 300 feet; trees debarked; steel-reinforced concrete structures badly damaged; asphalt roads sucked off the ground

Somewhere over the rainbow...

Chapter 7
HAIL

HOW DOES HAIL FORM?

Thunderstorms have winds that blow down out of the clouds toward the ground. They are called *downdrafts*. Thunderstorms also have winds that blow up into the clouds. They are called *updrafts*. If a raindrop gets caught in an updraft and is tossed into the coldest region of the cloud, it can be frozen. This is what hail is. Each time the frozen drops go up and down, they can get coated with more water and the hail gets bigger and bigger. Finally when the winds going up into the clouds aren't strong enough to keep the hail up in the air, the hail falls to the earth. Most hail is about the size of a pea, but hail can get bigger—much bigger.

RUDY WAS THE FIRST to see the lightning bolt that came from the dark, black clouds in the southwest sky. "Not again!" cried Rudy.

"What is it?" the others asked.

"I think there's another storm coming. Look over there."

Bryan said, "That does look like another big storm, but it looks different from the last one we were in."

"Different how?" asked Olivia.

"Well, see how it looks like a white curtain right in the middle of the large black cloud?" asked Bryan.

"Is that good or bad?" asked Rudy.

Bryan said, "The last storm didn't have that, but I don't think it's a good sign. I think it's a hail streak."

"You mean we're going to have hail?" asked Olivia.

Just then the first drops of rain from the approaching storm came splashing down. The raindrops were large and cold, and Rudy just knew there was going to be trouble.

"We'd better take shelter again," said Bryan.

weather FACT:

Largest Hail in the U.S.
circumference: 18.75 inches (distance around its surface)
diameter: 7.0 inches (length through the center from one side to the other side)
weight: nearly 1 pound
estimated impact speed: 100 mph
Aurora, Nebraska
June 22, 2003

Yikes!

They all headed back to the basement. The lights were still out, so the motel clerk led them down the dark stairs with his flashlight. This time there was no TV to watch, so they just closed the door and went to the walls of the basement. Olivia lifted some of the patio chairs off the stack and set them along the wall. Everyone sat down and waited quietly for the next storm. It didn't take long before they heard the booming thunder and howling wind.

"This must be the storm the TV weatherman showed on his radar that was southwest of here," said Bryan. Suddenly they heard a banging. It was like a slow knocking sound.

"Is that someone at the door?" asked Rudy.

"I don't know what it is," answered Bryan.

Olivia went up the stairs and was going to open the door. Then somebody or something knocked on the door just as she grabbed hold of the doorknob.

"Who's there?" Olivia called. Nobody answered.

There were two more knocks. Olivia slowly opened the door and peered into the motel lobby. Just then something whizzed right past her and clunked down the stairs into the basement. Rudy was so afraid he was frozen in his tracks. Bryan asked the motel clerk to shine the light on whatever it was. There in the beam of the flashlight was an egg, or at least it *looked* like an egg!

"That's a hailstone," cried Bryan. "It's a giant hailstone."

"You ought to see it out here," shouted Olivia from the top of the stairs.

One by one, they all crept up the stairs and peered out at the storm. Giant chunks of ice were pelting down with the heavy rain. Many of the hailstones were the size of chicken eggs and a few were even larger. There was a terrible racket as the stones clattered onto the parking lot and into what was left of the motel lobby. The storm went on for fifteen minutes before the hail finally quit. Outside, the hail was half a foot deep. It looked like there had been a snowstorm but no snow ever caused damage like this.

As the sky cleared, the Weather Detectives went into the parking lot to look around. There were dent marks all over the cars. It looked like someone had taken a hammer to them. "Do you think our car will still work?" asked Rudy.

"Oh, I'm sure it will," said Bryan. "We'll just need to get a new windshield."

Question

If a two-pound chunk of ice was falling from a thunderstorm, how fast would it be traveling when it hit the ground?

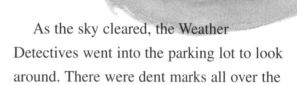

Caught you doing almost 100 in a 25 zone!

Answer

Very close to 100 miles per hour!

Chapter 8
NORTHERN LIGHTS

WHAT ARE THE NORTHERN LIGHTS?

Imagine that a wood-burning stove is the sun. Every so often when the fire is burning, a hot spark flies off. The sun is like this. The sun has hot spots that erupt and cause particles to fly off into space. If Earth happens to be in the way, then things can get exciting.

Earth has a magnetic field that surrounds it, so particles from space get guided in toward the North or South Poles. Things get exciting when the particles from the sun hit the upper layers of Earth's atmosphere. The different gases in the atmosphere light up when they are hit by the particles from the sun. For example, oxygen lights up either red or green and nitrogen lights up blue. The particles from the sun come more like a stream than like an ember, so the sky lights up with curtains of color. After a few minutes the stream of particles shifts or dies down and the display changes.

BRYAN, RUDY, AND OLIVIA'S next weather adventures were in Devil's Lake, North Dakota. The friends went there for a little trip to visit Bryan's Grandpa Bronson.

When they first arrived they saw a wiry old man sitting in a wooden rocking chair on the porch. Olivia thought to herself that Grandpa Bronson looked just like Bryan, only a lot older. He was of average height, was slender, and had the beginning of a gray beard.

Grandpa asked them about all their weather adventures, and they had a lot to tell! After dinner, Rudy, Olivia, Bryan, and Grandpa Bronson sat around talking. Later Bryan went for an evening walk. All of a sudden Bryan came running into the living room and hollered, "Hey guys, grab your coats and come with me. You've got to see this!"

"Is it good or bad?" asked Rudy rather fearfully.

"It's good," answered Bryan. "Come on!"

They all ran outside. The snow that had been falling earlier had quit and the night sky was clear. Bryan pointed to the north-

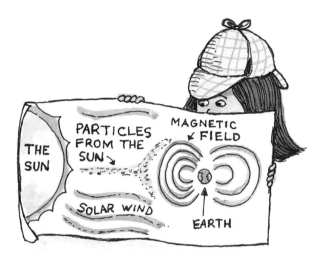

ern part of the sky and said, "Look at that!"

The sky had what looked like curtains of color. Some curtains were red and pink and others were green. The colored areas weren't really moving but after a few minutes the colors would change. Some colors in the sky would fade while others got brighter.

"It's the northern lights!" said Olivia. They stood in the cold watching the beautiful sight until they were so cold they had to go back inside.

"The real name for that beautiful display is the *aurora borealis*" (uh-ROAR-uh bohr-ee-AL-iss), said Bryan, "but everybody just calls it the northern lights."

"They happen a lot this far north," said Grandpa, "but you probably don't see the northern lights much in Florida or California."

"The reason we don't see the northern

lights that far south," explained Bryan, "is because they normally appear only in the polar regions."

Grandpa knew how smart Bryan was. He said, "Bryan, I've seen the northern lights quite a few times up here in North Dakota, near the Canadian border, but I don't recall seeing them very often when I lived in Kansas or Virginia. What causes them, and what makes the colors appear like that in the sky?"

"Well," said Bryan, "the northern lights are caused by hot spots erupting from the sun. When the eruptions on the sun are especially energetic, the display of the northern lights will be farther south. Occasionally, they can be seen as far south as Florida, but that's pretty unusual. There is a sunspot cycle that takes about eleven years. The display of northern lights goes through this same cycle.

Just then there was a popping sound like a firecracker from the wood-burning stove. A glowing ember shot out of the stove and landed on Rudy. "Yiiiiee!" he hollered as he jumped up and started dancing around. Finally the ember burned out.

"That's a good example," said Bryan.

"What's a good example?" stammered Rudy, as he sat back down again.

"That's a good example of the northern lights. When a spark from the fireplace lands on you, you get excited, just like when a hot spot from the sun hits Earth's atmosphere, things get excited."

Everyone laughed and Rudy grinned sheepishly.

Chapter 9

ICE

DURING THE NEXT TWO DAYS the temperature fell to ten degrees below zero. It was too cold to spend much time outside, but the kids did go out to the barn with Grandpa Bronson to help him feed the horses. On the way back to the house, Grandpa asked the kids how they would like fresh, panfried fish for dinner. They thought that would be great but couldn't

imagine where he would get fresh fish when it was ten degrees below zero.

That afternoon they all piled into Grandpa's old truck and he drove them down to a pond at the end of the pasture. The skies were blue and there wasn't much wind, but it sure was cold. The pond was frozen solid. Grandpa stopped the truck and told the kids to stay put. He got out and

Thickness of Ice

2 inches	Will normally hold one person
3 inches	Will hold several people walking single file
4 inches	Will safely hold a group of people
7 inches	Will hold a car
10 inches	Will hold a truck

found an ice drill in a toolbox in the back of the pickup. He walked out onto the ice and started drilling. The drill inched its way down into the ice as Grandpa turned the handle. After a few minutes he came back to the truck, put it in gear, and started driving out onto the pond.

Rudy screeched, "Oh, no!"

Olivia asked, "Are you sure it's safe to do this?"

Grandpa said, "I wouldn't drive us out here if it wasn't safe."

"But how do you know?" asked Rudy.

"Look in the glove box for a blue-colored card," said Grandpa. Rudy opened the glove box and found the card. It listed different thicknesses of ice and what they would safely hold.

"The ice is 12 inches thick, so we'll be

HOW DOES ICE FORM?

Many things get smaller when they are frozen, but not water. Water expands as it freezes. It is this unique property that lets us go ice skating on a pond. When a lake or pond freezes, the ice is lighter than the water, so the ice stays on top. A lake will freeze from the top down. As the temperature of water gets close to freezing (32 degrees Fahrenheit) the water molecules move a tiny bit apart from each other. Then when the temperature reaches 32 degrees, ice crystals begin to form, which locks the molecules into place. This is how ice is formed.

Lake ice freezes from the top down.

just fine," said Grandpa.

"I sure hope so," Rudy worried.

Grandpa stopped the truck about twenty feet out onto the pond. Everyone got out and watched Grandpa as he drilled another hole and started fishing. In a few minutes he caught a nice big fish, then another and another until he had plenty for dinner.

"That's it," he said, "we've got enough fish to fill up you kids." With that, he drove back to the ranch house and started cooking a most delicious dinner. The next day the Weather Detectives headed home.

weather FACT:
Coldest recorded place on earth
-129 degrees
Vostok, Antarctica
July 21, 1983

47

Chapter 10

FALLING
THROUGH A STORM

RUDY, OLIVIA, AND BRYAN were all sitting at home in the weather clubhouse. "I just read the most amazing story," Olivia said. "I've been searching through books and websites for stories about the weather. But this is unbelievable. It's about a guy who actually fell through a storm."

"What do you mean?" asked Rudy.

"I mean he jumped out of an airplane during a storm. The storm kept him from landing. He was being thrown around in the air for forty-five minutes, but somehow he lived to tell about it!"

"That's incredible!" said Bryan. "Read it to us."

So Olivia read the story out loud.

Back when I was in my twenties, I was a jet fighter pilot in the Marines. I was stationed in Virginia, and one day I was flying my jet on a training mission. It was a simple flight, and I was dressed in my lightweight flight suit. Everything was going fine until somewhere over Norfolk, Virginia, my engine quit. Now that is a very bad thing to happen when you are in a jet. If you are driving a car along the highway and the engine quits, you can pull over to the side of the road and try to get it fixed. When you are in a jet up in the sky and the engine quits, it is a different story—especially if you only have one engine like I did.

What you have to do is dive the aircraft and try to restart the engine. I tried that but it didn't work, so here I was headed to the ground like a rock. I hit the ejection button and the next thing I knew I was outside the aircraft. I was sitting in the cockpit one minute with a temperature around 70 degrees, and the next minute I was outside, nine miles above the ground, where it was 70 degrees *below zero*.

My parachute was set to open automatically when I reached two miles above the ground. So here I was, falling through the sky, half freezing to death, waiting for my chute to open. I fell for nearly four minutes! Think about that. It doesn't sound very long, but if you sit and watch your clock for four minutes you will see how long it is. Think about how it would make you feel if you fell and kept falling for that long. I fell seven miles through the air.

That was bad enough, but little did I know what was really in store for me. It turns out I had bailed out over a monster thunderstorm and I fell into it! When my parachute opened the winds immediately started blowing me back up into the storm! Then I started falling again. Up and down, up and down I went. Sometimes the parachute would cover me and I didn't think it was going to open again, but it did. Once after I was wrapped in the parachute, it opened off to the side of me and yanked me in that direction.

On two occasions, the parachute and I were doing loop-de-loops in the storm. It was like a nightmare, only it was real!

Then came the hail. Big chunks of ice hitting me here and hitting me there. I couldn't escape or hide—all I could do was hang on and hope it would quit. I didn't know it at the time, but my body was being bruised by the hammering of the hailstones.

Then I went through a rain area in the clouds that was unbelievable. It started raining so hard I actually had to hold my breath to keep from drowning! It was like being in a waterfall. It's funny the things that go through your mind at a time like that, but I wondered what people would think if they found my parachute hanging in a tree with me still strapped into the chute with my lungs full of water. Nobody would believe that I had drowned on the way down. I was drenched, beat up, half drowned, and I kept being tossed around by the winds in the storm.

After that there was lightning! Not just little streaks off in the distance—these were huge slabs of electricity. They came right next to me, and once it looked like the lightning went right between my legs. The lightning was sometimes a bluish color and looked like it was several feet thick. You've heard thunder before, but you've never heard anything like I heard! The sound was absolutely deaf-

ening. Each time a bolt of lightning went by there was an immediate boom of thunder that shook my body right down to the bones. In fact, if I hadn't been wearing my pilot's helmet, I probably would have lost my hearing. As it was, the sound broke one of my eardrums.

That storm tossed me up and down, my parachute opened and collapsed, the rain beat on me, lightning almost got me, and the thunder tried to deafen me, but I was still there. Finally, I could see the ground, but it was really windy and I knew I would have trouble landing. As I hung on under the parachute, I didn't have any way to steer. The newer parachutes today let you steer a little, but mine was one of the old ones and I had no control. Finally my chute got snagged in some tree branches and I slammed into the trunk of the tree.

I was exhausted and bruised and sore and nearly frozen, but I was alive. Normally it takes thirteen minutes to reach the ground when you bail out from that altitude, but it took me forty-five minutes. For three quarters of an hour I was in that storm being beat up. I was never so glad to see the ground in all my life. They tell me I landed sixty-five miles from where I had bailed out. I staggered over to a road where a passing truck picked me up and took me to town.

Based on the true story of Colonel William H. Rankin

"Wow," said Rudy. "What a story! I would have been so afraid."

"Now that's an amazing weather adventure," said Bryan.

Chapter 11
SNOW

WHERE DOES SNOW COME FROM?

Water has three different states. One state is liquid. A glass of water is water in the liquid state. Another state is frozen. An ice cube is water in the frozen state. The last state is vapor. Vapor is water (moisture) in the air. You can feel it, but you can't see it until certain things happen. Water is made of two hydrogen atoms and one oxygen atom. We call that H_2O. As water vapor freezes, the atoms join up in a way that makes six sides. Ice crystals are six sided, and as more water vapor freezes to the

crystal several different shapes are formed. The shapes depend on the temperature of the air. As each crystal forms it grows differently than any other. Just like there are no two fingerprints exactly the same, there are no two ice crystals exactly the same. A snowflake can be a single crystal, but it is usually made up of a collection of crystals. Some of the largest snowflakes occur when the temperature is very close to freezing.

THE WEATHER DETECTIVES were off on an adventure in Montana. They wanted to check out a place with a lot of snow. They found a place near Butte called the Snowslide Inn. Little did the three friends know that they were about to have an experience with an avalanche. What would Rudy think?

Adjoining the inn was a ski resort. Early in the morning, skiers and snowboarders were lined up to be first on the slopes. The storms of the previous week had brought more than three feet of new snow to the area, and the snowboarders were especially excited to try it out.

The ski patrol had checked out the area just after first light. The good news was that the ski area itself was in good shape

FACT or fiction?

Some outdoorsmen in snowy areas say that wasps will build their nests higher in the trees when an extra-snowy winter is coming.

and all ski runs were listed as safe and open. The bad news was that the backcountry was very dangerous with a high risk of avalanches. The ski patrol posted CLOSED AREA signs at all the appropriate places. While Bryan and his friends were having breakfast, a snowboarder was about to violate all the rules and go into the closed area of the mountain.

The snowboarder saw the signs that said the area was closed but was tempted by the deep snow that was untouched by any other skiers. The slope was pretty steep, and there were no trees, just a big, open bowl. Away he went, swooshing and turning down the steep slope. What a blast! But no sooner had he started than he heard a "whump" sound just behind him. As he looked over his shoulder, fear gripped his entire body. His heart beat in great thumps, pounding his chest, as he saw the wall of snow building behind him.

What should he do? What could he do? In school they had talked about avalanches, but what was he supposed to do? Try to outrun it, he thought, and he angled for the edge of the bowl. He couldn't go fast enough though, and now he could feel the snow dropping on the back of his neck. Then he remembered that he should try to stay on top.

As the snow closed in around him, he started moving his arms as if he were swimming. Furiously, frantically he moved his arms and tried to stay at the top of the churning snow where he could see the light.

As he was fighting for his life, he kept thinking, "Why did I go alone? Why didn't I go with my friends? Why did I go past the closed area signs?"

He rolled, tumbled, and twisted for

what seemed like forever. When the snow quit tumbling, it was going to turn almost as hard as concrete. He probably wouldn't be able to dig his way out. He would have to make a space so he could breathe and wait for someone to rescue him. All he could see was white and he couldn't tell if he was right-side-up or upside down. He thought it seemed brighter above him, as if that were the direction toward the sun and sky, so he thrust his hand upward toward the light.

Bryan, Olivia, and Rudy were in the restaurant just finishing their pancakes. As she sat at the breakfast table, Olivia was looking out the window at the beautiful day. She could see the snow-covered hills, and the sky was big and blue. Suddenly something caught her eye. She could see trees shaking and wiggling as if some giant wind were blowing them. Then she saw what looked like a white cloud moving rapidly along the ground. Somebody in the restaurant screamed "Avalanche!"

The avalanche was churning and plowing its way directly toward the restaurant. There were screams, then the crash of glass, and then a terrible noise as the wall of the restaurant collapsed. The snow rolled to within three feet of where the kids were eating their

weather FACTS:

Record snowfall in 12 months
1,140 inches
Mt. Baker, Washington
July 1998 to June 1999

Record snowflakes
15 inches in diameter
Fort Keough, Montana
January 28, 1887

Record snowfall in 24 hours
76 inches
Silver Lake, Colorado
April 14–15, 1921

breakfast!

Bryan, Rudy, and Olivia watched as the ski patrol rushed a few feet up the mountain from them. They started digging furiously. "What's going on?" asked Rudy.

"I think someone is buried under there," Olivia said. "Just before the avalanche quit moving I thought I saw an arm and a hand with a red glove. I think somebody is trapped under the snow!"

The kids ran up to see if they could help the ski patrol. Soon they heard faint cries from under the snow. As the men kept digging, they found the snowboarder with his body twisted up in the snow.

Before long they had the young man out of the snow and lying on the ground. He was scared, he was stiff and sore, but he was all right. No broken bones and no cuts, just some scrapes and bruises.

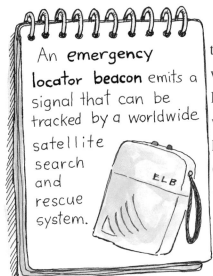

An **emergency locator beacon** emits a signal that can be tracked by a worldwide satellite search and rescue system.

A ski patrol officer asked the snowboarder if he was wearing an emergency locator beacon. He said he wasn't. The officer told him he was very, very lucky. Only one in three avalanche victims ever survives without a locator beacon.

As Rudy walked toward the car he was still shaking from the experience. "Let's go back to Mars," he said. "It was a lot safer there!"

Snowflakes or Pizzas?

The biggest known recorded snowflakes were 15 inches in diameter. Some people said they were the size of dinner plates. Others said they looked like giant white pizzas falling from the sky.

How could snowflakes get that big? What would be happening to allow that?

One theory—and this is just a theory—is that some snowflakes develop an electrical property that makes them act as a magnet for other snowflakes. The electrified snowflakes actually collect other snowflakes as they fall toward earth, so the original snowflake gets bigger and bigger. If there is a lot of wind, the giant snowflakes can get broken up again, but if there is little or no wind, the flakes keep getting bigger all the way to the ground.

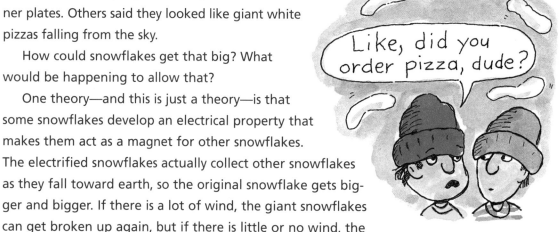

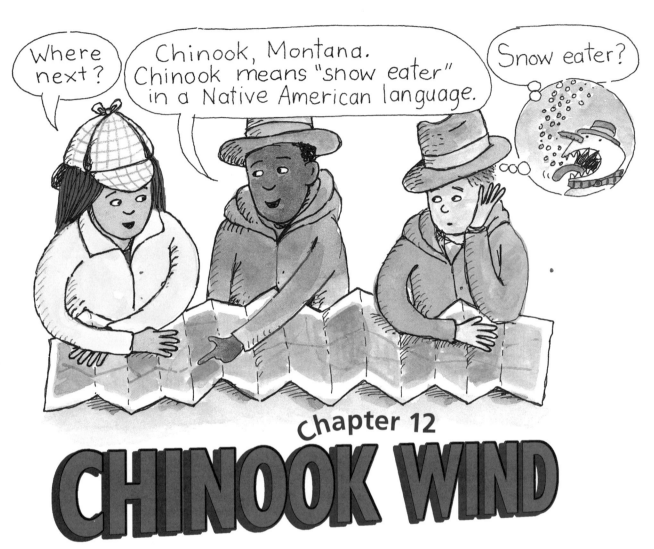

Chapter 12

CHINOOK WIND

THE TRICKY PART ABOUT WIND is that you can't see it. You can feel it, and you can see the things it blows around, but you can't actually see the wind itself. To get a better idea of how the wind works, think about it as water. The wind is like a river, only a very wide river. Some rivers move very fast, and some rivers move very slow. Think about the rivers you have

seen that were moving very fast. You were probably in or near the mountains where the land wasn't flat. The steeper the mountain, the faster the river flows. The flatter the ground, the more slowly the river flows.

Now imagine there are mountains in the sky. Actually there *are* mountains and valleys in the sky, but they are made of air, not rocks and dirt. In some areas, air from high in the atmosphere sinks toward the ground. The air flows downward faster than it can move away, so a mountain of air is formed. We can't see these mountains and valleys of air with our eyes, but the wind is caused by air flowing from the mountains of air into the valleys of air.

The mountains of air are called *high pressure areas* and the valleys of air are called *low pressure areas*.

THE SNOW EATER

The next day Rudy, Olivia, and Bryan left the Snowslide Inn to find another place to stay in Montana. It was bitter cold, and they were glad they had dressed warmly. When they looked at the car thermometer, it said 40 degrees below zero!

They got as far as Chinook, Montana, and thought they better get a motel and spend the night. Bryan told them it is dangerous to travel when it gets that cold. If you have something as minor as a flat tire, you can freeze to death trying to change it.

After they had dinner, Bryan put on his heavy coat and went to the registration desk at the motel. He asked the clerk if she had a yardstick he could borrow. Then he went outside to measure how deep the snow was. He made a path through the snow into what was the lawn area around the motel. He put the yardstick into the snow and pushed it down until it stopped when it hit the frozen ground. The snow was 24 inches deep. Bryan took out his pocket thermometer and took a reading. It

DID YOU KNOW?

How heavy do you think air is?
A postage stamp is about one inch on each side. If you took all of the air above this stamp, clear up to the top of the atmosphere, how much do you think it would weigh?

A column of air that tall would weigh 15 pounds! Air does have weight, and air rushing from high pressure areas to low pressure areas can cause strong winds.

was 50 degrees below zero. He went back into the motel and returned the yardstick. He was glad to be inside again where it was warm.

"How much snow is there?" asked Olivia.

"Twenty-four inches," responded Bryan. "And the snow really crunches when you walk on it."

"Is there any wind?" asked Rudy.

"No, it's just clear and cold—50 degrees below zero," answered Bryan.

"Fifty below zero!" they both said. "Holy cow!"

During the night, while they were all sleeping, the wind started blowing. At first the wind was bitter cold, but soon it began getting warmer. It was as if someone had turned on a giant hair dryer and held it on the town. Just before dawn, Rudy was awakened by what sounded like an explosion outside his motel window. He looked outside, but it was still dark and he couldn't see anything.

"That didn't sound good, whatever it was," thought Rudy, but then he went back to sleep.

In the morning when the sun came up,

DID YOU KNOW?

When you step on snow, your weight causes pressure that warms the snow slightly and allows the ice crystals to slide by each other rather quietly. When it is VERY cold the crystals don't slide easily. Instead they break, making a "crunching" sound. When snow crunches when you walk on it, it often means the temperature is very cold.

Olivia was first to notice. "How deep did you say the snow was?" Olivia asked Bryan at breakfast.

"Twenty-four inches. That's two feet deep," said Bryan.

"Well, not anymore," said Olivia. Bryan and Rudy looked out the window and couldn't believe their eyes. Outside there was only about an inch of snow on the lawn and there was water everywhere. It was from all the melted snow.

"That's impossible!" said Rudy.

Bryan took his pocket thermometer and ran outside to take a temperature reading. He could tell by the way the air felt on his face that it was much, much warmer than last night. His thermometer read 51 degrees *above* zero. "Could that be right?" he asked himself. He took another reading, but it was the same. He walked back into the motel.

"What's happening?" asked Rudy. Bryan told them the temperature was now 51 degrees and that was why the snow had melted.

"Wait a minute," said Olivia. "I thought you said it was 50 degrees *below* zero last night."

"I did," said Bryan. "Can you believe it?"

"You can't mean the temperature has risen over 100 degrees since yesterday?"

That's a tree?! Looks like a hot dog that got roasted too long!

asked Olivia.

As the three of them peered out the window of the motel lobby, they could see people walking around outside with short-sleeve shirts on. "What is going on?" Rudy asked the motel clerk.

"It's called a Snow Eater," the clerk said. "That's what the Chinook Indians of Montana call a warm winter wind like this."

"Well, it certainly ate last night's snow," said Olivia.

The clerk said this was the greatest temperature change she had ever seen. Then she asked them if they heard the noise in the night. Rudy said he had heard what sounded like an explosion. "Well, go outside and look at the tree on the north side of the motel," she said. When they went outside to look, they found the tree was split open like a hot dog that had been

weather FACT:

Record temperature change in 24 hours
103 degrees
Loma, Montana
low: −54
high: 49
January 14–15, 1972

roasted too long. They went back in and asked the clerk what had happened to the tree. She told them the temperature had changed so quickly in the night that the tree had exploded!

Rudy didn't say anything, he just thought to himself, "Giant snowflakes, exploding trees—I'm afraid to think what's next!"

A man came into the office and said he had just driven from Cut Bank, Montana, where the winds were blowing over 100 miles per hour. Olivia said there must be a monster storm coming with a wind like that. The man told them the skies were clear when he left; it was just very, very windy. The motel clerk said, "That's a Chinook wind."

"A Chinook wind?" they asked.

The clerk explained that very powerful

How Do Barometers Work?

pointer

lever

vacuum chamber

RAIN
CHANGE
FAIR

Most barometers today are called *aneroid barometers.* Inside there is a little metal container that looks like two small saucers on top of each other. One is facing up and the other is facing down, so there is a hollow space between them. As the weight of the atmosphere gets heavier, the air pushes down and the device collapses a tiny bit. When the atmosphere gets lighter the device expands a little bit. There is a pointer connected to the device that moves back and forth to show whether the air pressure is high or low.

When the air pressure is very high it usually means there is good, mild weather. When the barometer goes very low, it usually means a storm is coming. The faster the pressure is changing, the faster the weather will change.

winds blow over the Rocky Mountains and across the Montana prairie several times a year. They are usually warm winds, at least compared to the winds from Canada, and they last a day or two without bringing any storminess.

The man said, "But I don't understand how the wind can be so strong. It almost blew me off the highway."

"I think I can explain," Bryan said. "Strong winds are formed from air moving from high pressure areas to low pressure areas."

"But how can you tell what kind of pressure is in the sky if you can't see it?" asked Rudy.

Bryan walked over to the motel lobby wall by the clerk's desk. "See this?" He pointed to a round thing hanging on the wall. "This is called a *barometer* (bu-RAH-muh-tur), and it measures the pressure of the air."

The clerk walked over and said, "I've worked here more than five years and I didn't know that was a barometer. I thought it was just a decoration."

Bryan said, "Most barometers today look like decorations. They usually don't measure the pressure in pounds, but in inches of mercury or in millibars. Those are just different ways to measure the weight or pressure of the atmosphere. Most television weather reports give the pressure of the air in inches of mercury."

EXPERIMENT

Take a small balloon and blow it up. Hold the mouth of the balloon closed with your thumb and finger. Is the air pressure inside the balloon higher or lower than the air pressure outside the balloon? Which way does air move? Does it move from high pressure to low pressure or from low pressure to high pressure?

Air moves from high pressure to low pressure. The air pressure is higher inside the balloon, so if you open the mouth of the balloon, it flows out.

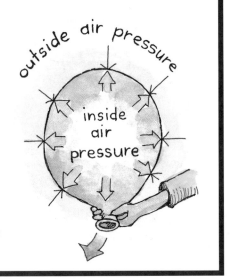

outside air pressure

inside air pressure

Chapter 13
LAKE EFFECT

WHAT IS THE LAKE EFFECT?

The lake effect is when cold air passes over the warm water of a lake and creates storminess. It's not quite that simple because other conditions have to be just right too, but the bottom line is that a lake can generate its own weather.

The weather caused by the lake effect can be very different than the weather that is right next to it. Sometimes there can be some really amazing amounts of storminess in a very small area. For example, sometimes a narrow band of weather can roll from the center of the lake to the shore like a blast from a fire hose. The storm can keep going and going for hours in the same place. At other times the lake effect is broad and will change the weather in an area along the shoreline for miles. It all depends on the winds, the temperature, and the moisture. The lake effect is almost like a miniature version of the water cycle.

BRYAN, OLIVIA, AND RUDY decided to take a trip to the Great Salt Lake. They knew there was often unusual weather in Salt Lake City and other nearby cities because of the lake effect. They decided to investigate and see what they could learn about the lake effect.

"Can you really float in the Great Salt Lake without sinking?" Olivia asked Bryan. Bryan had been to the Great Salt Lake once before.

"You can," replied Bryan. "The water levels in the lake go up and down

You can float in the Great Salt Lake because the salt makes the water more dense. In other words, the water is heavier than you, so you float.

weather FACT:

The Great Salt Lake in Utah is the largest lake in the United States other than the Great Lakes. It is so big you can see it from outer space. The Great Salt Lake often creates its own weather called the lake effect.

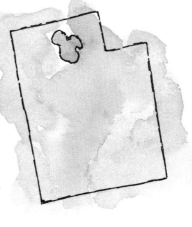

depending on how much rain and snow falls over the years, so the salt content of the lake goes up and down too. When the lake elevation is low, the water is six times saltier than the ocean and you can bob around like a cork."

Bryan's uncle was driving them out toward the lake. Suddenly Olivia told them to look at what was ahead. They saw a wall of thick, dark clouds with lightning bolts flashing. The weather had been really nice all the way from the airport, with just a few clouds when they arrived in Utah. But now, near the town of Bountiful, Utah, a storm was coming off the lake and rolling eastward into the mountains. As

How the
LAKE EFFECT
causes snow

COLD AIR

COOL AIR

WARM LAKE

DID YOU KNOW?

In the very high elevations of the Rocky Mountains is a small animal called a pika (PIE-ka). The pika doesn't hibernate, so it has to gather food during the summer to last it through the winter. They make little "haystacks" that get buried in the snow. The pika then goes back and forth from its borough to its haystack to get food in the winter. Mountain men say the bigger the haystack, the harder the coming winter will be.

they got closer Bryan exclaimed, "I know what that is! It's a lake effect storm in action!"

Olivia and Rudy got out their notebooks.

Suddenly the car was swallowed up in a blinding snowstorm. It may have been spring, but the Great Salt Lake was making it look like winter. In less than a mile, they went from a dry road to a road covered with snow. It was surprising to say the least! The snowflakes were large and thick and pelted their car with a fury.

"Do you think we should pull off and stop?" asked Olivia.

Bryan said, "No, let's keep driving, but go slowly."

It was hard to drive because they couldn't see the white lines on the road. The snow was now three or four inches deep and there was another bolt of lightning. "Lightning and snow together," thought Rudy. "How weird." After seven more miles the snow was getting lighter. In another mile the snow quit, and then the road was dry. Their investigation had certainly been worth it. They had experienced the lake effect before they even got to the shores of the Great Salt Lake!

Chapter 14

TEMPERATURE

AFTER A BRIEF STAY IN SALT LAKE CITY, the Weather Detectives decided on a trip to Bryce Canyon to see the famous red rock formations. They headed out on their trip, deciding to stop for the night in Beaver, Utah. They pulled into the Dew Drop Inn and unloaded the car.

That evening they were sitting on the porch looking up at the stars. There was a chorus of crickets coming from some nearby bushes, and the evening was very relaxing. The kids were talking about their trip to Bryce Canyon the next day.

A local man walked up and greeted

them. "Evenin', kids!" he said. "It's a mighty nice night out here. My name is Orsen Buggy. Welcome to Beaver."

"Good evening," the kids replied. Bryan asked the man if he knew what time it was. Mr. Buggy looked at his watch.

"It's 9:30," he said.

Rudy spoke up. "It sure seems warm for this time of night."

The old-timer looked back at his watch and started counting softly to himself. Rudy looked at Olivia and Olivia looked at Bryan. They all shrugged their shoulders as Mr. Buggy continued counting.

Finally he announced, "It's 70 degrees right now, and that makes it very pleasant."

Rudy's face twisted up a bit. He asked, "It's 70 degrees right now? Right here? How do you know that?"

Mr. Buggy laughed and sat down on the porch next to the kids. "It's the crickets," he said. "They're

smart. They know the temperature."

Now Rudy looked really confused. "Crickets?" he asked. "What do the crickets have to do with the temperature?"

"Crickets do their chirping according to the temperature of the air. Bugs are a lot different from people or most animals, you know. People and animals keep their body temperature pretty even, but the body temperature of bugs changes with the air temperature," Mr. Buggy explained.

"The crickets do a little singsong at night to call to other crickets," he continued. "If the night is warm, the crickets' bodies are

EXPERIMENT

Crickets do most of their chirping at night and usually don't chirp much when the temperature gets below 50 degrees. How would you like to make a cricket-temperature formula for the crickets in your neighborhood? All you need is a thermometer, a watch, and a connection to the Internet.

You will need to keep a record of the crickets' chirps when the night is cool, when it is warm, and when the temperature is in between. Take your thermometer with you and get fairly close to where the crickets are chirping. Use your watch and count the number of chirps in 60 seconds. Write that number down and next to it record the current temperature. Do this for at least three different temperatures, preferably with some readings in the low 60s, some near 70, and some near 80. The more readings the better.

chirp

Only male crickets chirp. They chirp by scraping their hind legs against their wings.

Once you have your readings, go to this website: www.gibbs-smith.com and click on The Weather Detectives. Then click on cricket formula. Follow the directions and it will give you a temperature formula to use for the crickets at your house. Once you have the formula, all you will have to do is count the number of chirps, use your formula, and amaze your friends!

warmer and they chirp faster. When the night is cool, the crickets' bodies are cooler and they chirp slower."

Rudy was still a little confused, but he kept listening. Mr. Buggy went on, "If you know how many chirps there are in a certain length of time, then you can tell the temperature."

Mr. Buggy told the kids that for most of one summer he had counted the cricket chirps for one minute then checked the air temperature with a thermometer. He then recorded that information on a graph. Some nights were warm and some nights were cool, and he faithfully recorded the temperature and the chirps. When he looked at the chart at the end of the summer, most of the points were along a line. Then by using a little math called algebra, he worked out a formula.

"Here's the formula I came up with. You count the number of chirps you hear in 13 seconds then add 40. That will tell you the temperature of the air."

Olivia exclaimed, "That's amazing!"

Rudy just shook his head and looked at Bryan. "Did you know that about crickets, Bryan?" he asked.

"I knew crickets were cold-blooded and chirped in response to the temperature," Bryan answered, "but I didn't know there was a way to figure out the temperature based on their chirps!"

Mr. Buggy said, "I told you kids. Those crickets are smart!"

Chapter 15

FLASH FLOODS

WATER IS CENTRAL to every kind of weather we have on Earth. Water from the oceans evaporates and turns into clouds, and the water in the clouds condenses into rain that falls back to Earth, as you learned in chapter 2. Rain, snow, and hail are all different forms of water falling to Earth. When rain falls faster than the ground can absorb it, it can cause a flash flood.

THE WEATHER DETECTIVES were on a sightseeing trip in Bryce Canyon National Park. Because they had already come to Utah to see the lake effect in action, they thought they should stay a few days longer to see the amazing sites at the national park. It was a little out of their way, but they wanted to see the red rock spires that looked so much like the landscape on Mars. They also knew the park was a site for flash floods. Rainwater can fill the narrow canyons and trails there quickly with nowhere else to go. The water can get so deep that people can drown. Flash floods are very dangerous, and the

FLASH FLOOD SAFETY RULES

✓ Go to high ground immediately. Get out of areas that may flood, including dips, low spots, canyons, and washes.

✓ Do not try to cross a flowing stream on foot where water is above your knees.

✓ Do not camp along streams and washes, particularly during threatening conditions.

✓ Do not play near storm drains or washes after a heavy rain.

kids hoped they didn't experience one, but it would be interesting to investigate the kinds of conditions that led to flash floods.

In the park, they came to a trail that led down into the canyon, and Bryan wanted to take a short hike. Just then a park ranger walked up and asked if they were going hiking. "Yes, we are," said Bryan. "Do you know which is the best trail to take?"

"I like the Peekaboo Loop trail the best," the ranger said. "But be careful. Pay attention to the skies because a flash flood watch has been issued."

"What do you mean *watch*," asked Rudy suspiciously.

"A *watch* means there is a possibility for flooding, but nothing is going to happen immediately. So just keep your eyes open," said the ranger. As the friends looked at the sky there wasn't a cloud to be seen. "How can there be a storm when there aren't any clouds around?" Rudy asked.

Bryan said, "I've heard things can change pretty fast around here."

Soon they were on the trail and walking among the giant red towers of sandstone. It was an amazing sight with the red earth, the blue skies, and the puffy little white clouds that were developing.

The kids sat by a fallen log and ate the

picnic lunch they had brought. They were now shaded from the sun by quite a few clouds as they sat talking and eating. All of a sudden—CRACK . . . BAM!

There was a blinding flash and a deafening roar as lightning hit a nearby tree. Rudy was up off the fallen log like he had been ejected from a plane. "Oh, no!" he cried. "We're going to be killed in a flash flood!"

"Slow down," said Bryan. "It's not a flood yet. But that lightning bolt was close. We better get right back to the lodge and take shelter."

As they all looked around at the sky, they noticed it had gotten very cloudy while they had eaten their lunch. It looked like rain clouds were in the distance and thunderstorms were building. They climbed the steep trail and were soon high enough to see the many thunderheads that had formed all around them. Lightning was flashing in several clouds. When they approached the lodge, the ranger was heading down the trail toward them.

"I was just coming to get you kids," he said. "The National Weather Service has now issued a flash flood warning for this area. We're going to close the hiking trails until it is safe again."

"You mean it's not safe *now*?" moaned Rudy, as they walked back to the lodge.

"It is safe, if we follow the safety rules," answered the ranger.

Just then a tremendous flash lit up the sky, followed by a huge boom that sounded like a bomb. They all looked at each other and the ranger said, "This is going to be quite a storm."

Back at the lodge, they peered out the window, but it was hard to see anything. The rain was coming down like a waterfall. There was a loud drumming sound as it beat on the roof. Water was running everywhere outside.

After several minutes, the rain quit. Soon they could see the red spires of Bryce Canyon again.

"How much rain do you think that storm

dropped?" Bryan asked the ranger.

"Let's go into the office and look at the rain gauge," he answered.

The three of them followed the ranger to his office. The ranger explained that there was an official rain gauge located outside the lodge that sent the rainfall readings to the computer on his desk.

"Let's see," the ranger said, as he scrolled down through the data. "Wow! We had 1.03 inches in 3 minutes. I've never seen that much rain in such a short time here. This is a new record for the state of Utah."

"This reminds me of another huge rainstorm we were in," Rudy said. The others agreed.

"Tell me about it," said the ranger.

"Well, we were driving through California and all of a sudden we could see large thunderclouds all around us. But it wasn't raining. Pretty soon it started getting dark, not because night was coming but because the clouds were so thick. I remember Bryan told us that when the clouds are extra thick and tall and are filled with raindrops, the light from the sun gets blocked so it looks almost dark."

"That's right," said Bryan.

"Anyway," Rudy continued, "soon enough, we drove right into a cloudburst. We could hardly see the road and the driver slowed down to just a crawl. The windshield wipers were going on high speed, throwing water off our windshield, but we

HEAD TO THE CAR!

Cars are usually a safe place to be during a lightning storm if you can't get inside a building. Convertibles aren't safe though, because they don't have a metal top. It is the metal that surrounds the car that helps make it safe. Many people think it is the rubber tires that make cars safe in a lightning storm. Actually, lightning is so powerful, it can jump right over the rubber tires. The real reason cars are safe is that lightning likes to go over the surface of objects, so if an all-metal car does get hit, the electricity tends to go over the metal shell and frame of the car and into the ground, rather than into the person!

still couldn't see very well. Then Bryan called out, 'Watch out, there's water across the road!' The driver stopped the car. We were in a low spot on the highway. It was hard to tell, but the water looked about a foot deep."

"Wow," said the ranger. "What did you do?"

"The driver slowly edged the car into the running water. Everything was fine. Then I looked out the window and could see pinecones and sticks and other stuff floating along in the muddy water. The water across the road was about twenty-five feet wide, and as we got to about the middle, the car started sliding to the left. I was scared! Our driver shifted the car to a lower gear and gave it a little more gas. The front of the car lurched forward but the back slid downstream a little more with the rushing water.

For a minute we were crooked in the road, but then the car pulled forward out of the flood."

"You're lucky you got through that okay," said the ranger. "Flash flooding on the road can be really dangerous."

"That wasn't the worst of it," said Rudy. "A few miles farther down the road the pavement was dry and we saw a dry streambed. People were camped right next to it, with tents and camp trailers. Bryan told our driver to turn into the camping area. He said we needed to warn those people about what was coming.

"Well, Bryan jumped out of the car and yelled to all the people that a flash flood was coming.

"An older man came up to Bryan and said, 'It isn't raining, so how could there

What Is a Thunderhead?

A thunderhead is a rounded bunch of cumulus (KEWM-yuh-luhs) clouds often appearing before a thunderstorm.

be a flash flood?' Bryan said it was raining like crazy not far from there and he thought all the runoff water was headed for their streambed.

"The older man ran back to the others and they took down the tents and loaded up in record time. Then they followed us up out of the dry streambed onto the paved highway. 'This is crazy,' said one of the men, as we pulled our cars to the side of the road and looked back at the perfectly dry streambed. Another man said, 'Let's go back and set up our camp again.'

"While they were talking about what they should do, we heard a sound. At first it was just a rumble, like thunder in the distance.

"Pretty soon the sound got louder and louder and we could hear a clicking, bonking sound. Now all of them had stopped talking and were looking in the direction of where the sound was coming. 'What's that?!' asked the older man. Just then a little kid hollered, 'Look at that!'

"From around a slight bend in the streambed water came rushing down. Tree branches and whole tree trunks were riding along in the muddy water. It was a wall of water! It was nearly ten feet high, and so powerful that it was moving rocks and boulders right out of its way!

"We just all stood there stunned as the flash flood roared down that old, dry streambed. I remember that old man looking over at Bryan. 'You saved our lives, kid,' he said. 'I don't know how to thank you.'"

"That's quite a story," the park ranger said.

WARNING SIGNS OF A FLASH FLOOD

✓ Very heavy rain falling in a short period of time
✓ Heavy rain falling on rocky ground
✓ Heavy rain falling on a deep snow cover
✓ Thunderstorms that sit over distant mountains for a long time
✓ A stream or river that keeps rising

Chapter 16

SUN

THE SUN, like water, supports all life on this planet. If the sun didn't exist, neither would we. The sun is the spoon that stirs our atmosphere. Without the sun, all the water on Earth would freeze and Earth would be a giant ball of ice. The sun is 93 million miles away, but we receive just the right amount of sunlight to keep our planet livable.

THE WEATHER DETECTIVES decided to visit Death Valley, California.

After all, it was one of the hottest places in America. The sun is so central to our weather, they wanted to observe what the weather would be like in those extreme conditions.

The friends got to Death Valley around 10:00 a.m. It was a sunny day and it was hot! They couldn't believe how hot it was for so early in the day. It was already 110 degrees. What would the afternoon bring?

The friends

Tips for Staying Safe in Extreme Heat

✓ Drink plenty of water.
✓ Wear sunscreen.
✓ Wear big hats to give you shade.
✓ Don't go hiking or exercise in extreme heat.
✓ Try to stay out of the sun as much as possible and keep cool.

DID YOU KNOW?

The sun is made of helium and hydrogen gas.

The sun is so far away it takes sunlight over 8 minutes to reach Earth!

The sun is so big that over one million Earths could fit inside it!

stopped by some large sand dunes near the highway. Rudy wanted to walk out on the dunes and have his picture taken. Bryan and Olivia stayed by the car as Rudy walked out on the sand. Suddenly Rudy was jumping and hopping and dancing around shouting, "Ow, ow, ow!"

"What's the matter?" shouted Olivia.

"The sand is so hot, it's burning my feet right through my shoes!" Rudy called back.

He ran back and got into the shade of the sand dunes sign. Bryan got a blanket out of the trunk of the car and quickly walked out where Rudy had been. He folded the blanket several times, threw it down, then stood on it. He took his pocket thermometer and put it about one inch into the sand. After a minute he called back, "Even with the blanket my shoes are getting really hot." Then he came running back to the car.

Olivia asked Bryan how hot the sand was. "Unbelievable," was his reply, "the sand temperature is 205 degrees!"

"Whoa!" said Olivia. "Water starts to boil at 212 degrees. Let's get out of here!"

weather FACTS:

Hottest place on earth
136 degrees
El Azizzia, Libya, Africa
September 13, 1922

Driest place on earth
0.03 inches rain each year
(59-year average)
Arica, Chile, South America
Arica once went for 40 years
without any rain!

CONCLUSION

WITH ALL THEIR DIFFERENT travel and adventures, news of the Weather Detectives started to get around. One day one of the network television news shows called the kids and asked if they could interview them. They asked Bryan about the world science fair and all about his trip to Mars. They asked Rudy and Olivia all about their weather experiments and amazing adventures.

Things went so well and people liked the show so much, that they asked the Weather Detectives to be a permanent part of the show. Once a month they would do a special presentation on the nightly news. That would keep them busy investigating to find new facts for interesting stories! The three friends decided they would never grow tired of learning new things about the weather.